# Contents

# Awesome paper

You can do so much more than just write on paper! There are lots of wonderful pieces of art that you can make from paper alone. In this book we'll show you how to make paper windmills, monster masks, party hats, cards, treasure chests and much, much more.

Find out just how awesome paper art can be!

# Awesome Art

# Paper Art

## Jeanette Ryall

raintree

a Capstone company — publishers for children

Raintree is an imprint of Capstone Global Library Limited, a company incorporated in England and Wales having its registered office at 264 Banbury Road, Oxford, OX2 7DY – Registered company number: 6695582

www.raintree.co.uk
myorders@raintree.co.uk

Produced for Raintree by Calcium
Edited by Sara Antill
Designed by Jeanette Ryall
Original illustrations © Capstone Global Library Limited 2020
Originated by Capstone Global Library Ltd
Printed and bound in India

978 1 3982 0032 6 (hardback)
978 1 3982 0037 1 (paperback)

British Library Cataloguing in Publication Data
A full catalogue record for this book is available from the British Library.

Acknowledgements
We would like to thank the following for permission to reproduce photographs: Cover: Jeanette Ryall l, Shutterstock Thomas M Perkins r. Inside: pp. 4–5: Tudor Photography; pp. 6–7 (main) Tudor Photography, (steps) Tudor Photography; pp. 8–9 (steps) Tudor Photography; p. 9 (main) Tudor Photography; pp. 10–11 (steps) Tudor Photography; p. 11 (main) Tudor Photography; pp. 12–13: (steps) Tudor Photography; p. 13: (main) Tudor Photography; p. 14 (main) Tudor Photography; pp. 14–15 (steps) Tudor Photography; p. 15 (main) Tudor Photography; pp. 16–17: (steps) Tudor Photography; p. 17 (main) Tudor Photography; p. 18 (steps) Tudor Photography; p. 19 (main) Tudor Photography; p. 20 (main) Jeanette Ryall; pp. 20–21 (steps) Tudor Photography; p. 21 (main) Tudor Photography; pp. 22–23 (steps) Tudor Photography; p. 23 (main) Tudor Photography; pp. 24–25 (steps) Tudor Photography; p. 25 (main) Tudor Photography; pp. 26–27 (steps) Tudor Photography; p. 27 (main) Tudor Photography; pp. 28–29 (steps) Tudor Photography; p. 29 (main) Tudor Photography.

Every effort has been made to contact copyright holders of material reproduced in this book. Any omissions will be rectified in subsequent printings if notice is given to the publisher.

All the internet addresses (URLs) given in this book were valid at the time of going to press. However, due to the dynamic nature of the internet, some addresses may have changed, or sites may have changed or ceased to exist since publication. While the author and publisher regret any inconvenience this may cause readers, no responsibility for any such changes can be accepted by either the author or the publisher.

# You will need:

All the items you will need for each activity are listed on the following pages in a "You will need" box, like this one. Read these boxes carefully before you start to make sure that you have everything you need.

## Before you start:

• Ask your parent or guardian for **permission** to use the equipment and space you will need for each activity.

• Find an apron to cover your clothes, or wear old clothes that you don't mind getting dirty.

• Ask an adult to help you with the activities that require cutting.

# Crawling caterpillars

## You will need:

- green and orange paper • scissors
- black pen
- two plastic eyes
- **pipe cleaner**
- glue • ruler

From a piece of green paper and a piece of orange paper, cut two strips about 20 cm long. Glue the two pieces together, as shown above. They should make an L shape. Leave them to dry.

2

## Top tip
You can make big or small **accordions** by changing the length and width of the paper.

Once the glue has dried, fold the green paper over the orange paper. Then fold the orange paper over the green paper. Repeat this pattern until you have reached the end of the strips of paper.

Glue the ends of the orange and green paper together. Once the glue has dried, gently pull out the accordion shape to make the body of your crawling caterpillar.

Glue the plastic eyes to one end of the caterpillar and draw on a smiling mouth. Take a pipe cleaner and cut off two pieces 5 cm long. Twist the ends of the pipe cleaners, then glue them onto the head of the caterpillar as shown below.

# Windy windmills

## You will need:

- colourful card
- paper fastener • scissors
- glue • straw
- sticky tape
- ruler

**Top tip**
Try decorating a windmill with **sequins** instead of paper.

**1** From the card, cut out a 20 cm square. Then cut out 20 small coloured squares. Glue them onto your large square in a **design**.

**2** Put a dot of glue into the centre of the square. Make a cut about 5 cm long into each of the four corners of your square. Fold in each of the corners.

**3**

When each corner is folded in, use some sticky tape to stick the tip of each corner to the centre of the windmill. This will ensure that the corners stay in position.

**4**

Use a paper fastener to fix the corners firmly to the centre of the windmill. Use sticky tape to attach the straw to the back of the windmill.

# Monster mask

## You will need:

- colourful card
- colourful feathers
- colourful **tissue paper**
- sequins • glue
- scissors

Using a sheet of card, cut a circle large enough to cover your face. Cut a slit in the circle, then fold it into a cone. Fix it into position with glue, then cut two holes for the eyes.

Cut 15 squares of multi-coloured card. Cut some short strips, too. Glue the strips along the top of the mask. Glue the squares on top of the strips to create a fringed effect.

## Top tip

**Ruffle** the edges of the squares to make them look like hair.

**3**

Take two sheets of colourful tissue paper and tear them into squares. Glue the squares from one colour in a triangular shape onto the top half of the mask. Glue the other squares onto the bottom half of the mask.

**4**

Cut out two triangular shapes for the nose and two **semicircles** for the eyebrows. Cut a red square for the mouth and two strips of jagged white paper for teeth. Glue these shapes to the mask. Add feathers and sequins.

# Paper flowers

## You will need:

- red and green paper • glue
- scissors • thick green pen
- green pipe cleaner
- small vase
- sand

Pour some sand into a small vase, then place your rose **stem** into the sand. This will keep it upright.

To make the rose bud, tear off two semicircles of red paper. Roll one piece of paper into a small **spiral** shape. Use glue to hold the shape in position.

To make your petals, cut out some small semicircles of red paper. Wrap a semicircle around your rose bud. Glue the ends together, then glue the petal to the bud. Repeat with each of your petals.

**3**

Cut out some large semicircles to make the outer petals. Wrap them around the rose bud and glue them into position, as you did in step 2. You have created your rose shape.

**4**

From green paper, cut out two leaf shapes. Use a green pen to draw the veins of the leaves. Glue the leaves to your rose. Glue the pipe cleaner to the rose to make a stem. Your rose is complete!

**Top tip**

To change the colour of your rose, just change the colour of the paper.

# Princess party hat

## You will need:

- pink card • dark pink and pale pink tissue paper
- glue • ruler
- scissors • silver and pink ribbon • sequins
- sticky tape

**1**

Roll a sheet of pink card into a cone shape. Seal the sides into position with sticky tape, leaving a small hole at the top.

**2**

From some dark pink and pale pink tissue paper, cut some small heart shapes. You will need about 20 heart shapes. Glue the hearts onto the cone to make a nice pattern.

## Top tip

You could make a wizard hat or a clown hat, too!

14

**3**

To add more decorations to your cone, glue on lots of sparkling sequins. Make sure that you cover every side, then leave it to dry.

**4**

Cut five pieces of both the silver and pink ribbon. They should be about 25 cm long. Feed the end of each piece into the hole at the top of the hat. Use sticky tape to fix the ribbon into position inside the hat.

# Monster mâché

## You will need:

- empty plastic bottle
- two empty juice cartons
- **variety** of paint colours
- sticky tape • flour
- glue • newspaper
- tissue paper
- paintbrush

For the monster's body, use the empty bottle. Crumple some newspaper into a large ball and tape it to the bottle. This will become the monster's head.

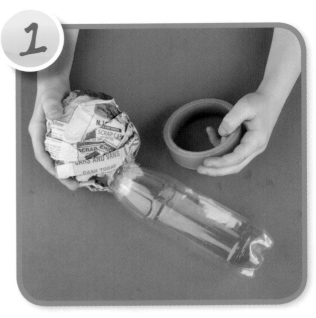

Cover the bottle in **layers** of newspaper and tape into position to make the monster's body. Cover the two empty juice cartons with newspaper to make the arms.

**3**

Tape the arms to the monster's body. To make the claws, roll six small pieces of newspaper into tiny cone shapes. Tape three cones onto the end of each arm.

**5**

Fix the feet to the **base** of the body with sticky tape. Point the feet outwards to make your monster stand up. Then roll up two small balls of newspaper for the eyes.

**4**

Roll some sheets of newspaper into two foot shapes, as shown. Attach to the body with sticky tape. Attach eight small cones of newspaper for the claws.

**6**

Tape the eyes to the top of the head. Mix flour and water into a thick, smooth paste. Tear lots of strips of newspaper. Cover the strips with the paste to make papier-mâché, then use to completely cover your monster.

**7**

Once you have coated your monster in lots of layers of papier-mâché, leave it overnight to dry. When the monster is completely dry, you can paint it.

**9**

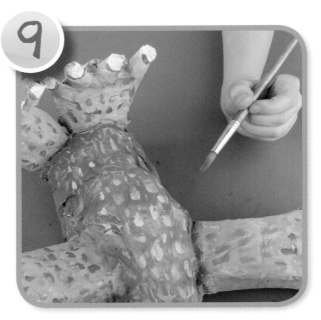

Paint the body a dark green, and the arms and feet a light green. Leave the paint to dry. Then paint a pattern onto your monster using yellow paint.

**8**

Cover the monster in white paint. You will need to paint it several times. Let each layer of paint dry before painting the next. This will stop the newspaper showing through.

**10**

Finally, paint the face of your monster. Add sharp, white teeth, a red mouth and crazy eyes. To make hair, **shred** some pieces of tissue paper and glue them onto the head.

## Top tip

You can make big
or little monsters
by using bottles of
different sizes.

# Daisy flowers

## You will need:

- white paper • thick yellow pen • green card
- pencil • scissors
- sticky tape • glue
- small coin

Draw 12 small circles onto a piece of paper. You can use the inside of a roll of sticky tape or you can draw around a circular shape, such as a small coin.

Carefully cut out the circles. Using a thick yellow pen, add a small dot to the middle of each circle so that they look like daisies.

**3**

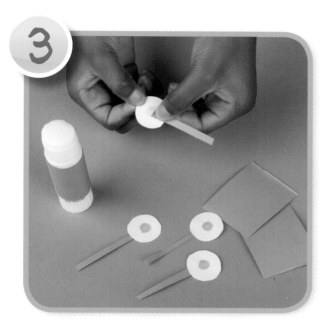

**Top tip**
Cut lines into several daisies at once to create lots of petals quickly.

Now cut out 12 thin strips from the green card. These are the stalks for your daisies. Glue a stalk to the back of each daisy.

**4**

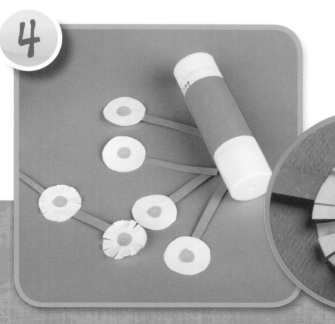

Take care not to cut too close to the centre of the daisy.

Cut small lines into the edge of each daisy to form the petals. Gently ruffle the cut parts of the white paper to create a petal effect.

# Cute cards

## You will need:

- white, yellow, pink, and orange card
- scissors • glue
- pencil • ruler
- black pen

**Top tip**
Use the same **technique** to make lots of different cards!

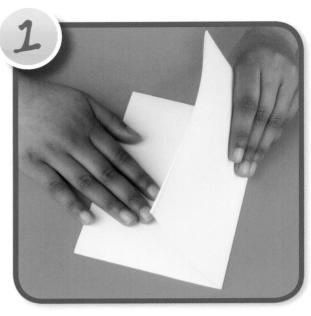

Fold a large sheet of white card in half. Then fold the paper in half again to make a greeting card.

On yellow card, draw the **outline** for a duck's head. Then cut it out. Cut a large diamond from orange card. Use the black pen to draw eyes onto white paper, then cut them out, too.

**3**

Fold back the top of the beak to make it open easily.

Fold the yellow and orange shapes in half. Glue both to the middle of the card, lining up the fold on each shape with the fold of the card. Glue on the eyes and cut a slit into the orange shape to make the beak.

**4**

Make a worm by cutting a length of pink paper 13 cm long. Cut out and glue on a small white circle for the worm's eye. Draw a black dot in the middle, and a mouth. Glue the worm to the inside of the beak.

# Pirate flags

## You will need:

- colourful paper
- scissors • ruler
- black pen • string
- sticky tape

## Top tip
Ask an adult to fix your flags to the walls of your bedroom.

**1** Cut 13-cm long strips from a variety of different coloured paper. Fold them all in half.

**2** Hold the folded edge of each strip and cut a V shape into the other end. Hold the paper strip flat as you cut so that both sides are cut.

**3**

Use a black pen to draw a design onto each strip. Draw designs such as pirate flags, **skull and crossbones**, **anchors** and stripes.

Make sure you draw a variety of designs onto your pirate flags.

**4**

Cut a length of string 51 cm long. Hang the folded edge of each flag over the string. Fix the flags in place with sticky tape.

**Top tip**
Try using pretty patterned paper for a different look.

# Treasure chest

## You will need:

- **tracing paper**
- blue card • glue
- scissors • pencil
- green tissue paper
- foil • ruler
- black pen
- cutting knife

**1**

Trace the chest pattern on page 28 onto a thin piece of blue card. Cut out the shape, then cut along the solid lines.

**2**

Ask an adult to **score** the dotted lines. Then fold the scored lines. You are creating all the folds you will need to make your chest.

**3**

Glue the back of the corner tabs marked 9, 10, 11 and 12 to the inside of the base ends. This will form the shape of the chest.

**5**

Cut two long strips of the foil paper about 2.5 cm wide. Draw bolts onto the strips, then glue them to the edges of the chest.

**4**

Glue the back of tabs 1, 2, 3 and 4 to the inside of the lid ends. Glue tabs 5, 6, 7 and 8 to the insides of the lid ends. This will complete the lid.

**6**

Copy the lock design from page 28 onto some foil. Cut it out and glue it to the chest. Create seaweed by gluing strips of green tissue paper to the chest, then fill with treasure.

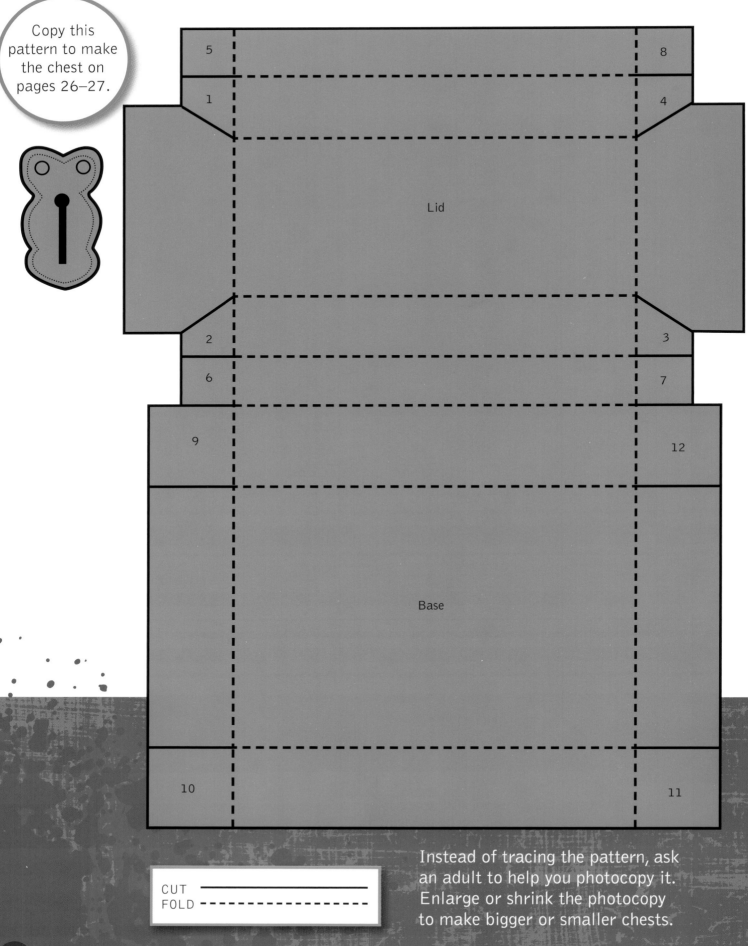

Copy this pattern to make the chest on pages 26–27.

5

8

1

4

Lid

2

3

6

7

9

12

Base

10

11

Instead of tracing the pattern, ask an adult to help you photocopy it. Enlarge or shrink the photocopy to make bigger or smaller chests.

CUT ———————
FOLD - - - - - - - - - - - -

**Top tip**
Store your jewels
or coins in your
treasure chest!

# Glossary

**accordions** objects with lots of folded sections. Accordions can be folded flat or opened out into long shapes

**anchors** heavy weights attached to a chain. Anchors are thrown from a boat or ship to hold it, or "anchor" it, to the seabed.

**base** bottom of something

**design** pattern or different shapes that make an image

**layer** sections that are placed on top of one another

**outline** outer line of a shape

**permission** allowed to do something

**pipe cleaner** length of thin wire covered in a soft material

**ruffle** lift the edges of something so that it is no longer flat

**score** make a light mark with a pair of scissors or knife

**semicircles** half circles

**sequins** small, shiny shapes used for decorating

**shred** tear roughly into thin strips

**skull and crossbones** design once used on pirate flags. It features a skull with two crossed leg bones.

**spiral** long, coiled shape

**stem** hard structure that holds a plant upright

**technique** way of doing something

**tissue paper** very thin, soft paper

**tracing paper** light, see-through paper

**variety** lots of different types of something

# Find out more

## Books

*Next Chapter Crafts: Page Turning Projects*, Jen Jones
and Marne Ventura (Raintree, 2018)

*Origami Crafting* (Origami Crafting 4D), Christopher Harbo
(Raintree, 2017)

*Start Your Crafting Business* (Build Your Business),
Mary Meinking (Raintree, 2017)

## Website

www.bbc.co.uk/cbbc/games/cbbc-picture-maker
Create your own digital pictures using paints, stickers, glitter and more.

# Index